# Louis Pappas New Generation Greek Cuisine

RECIPES
LOUIS PAPPAS

PHOTOGRAPHY
CHARLES EANES

FOOD STYLIST
NANCY PAPPAS

EDITOR
SUSAN EANES

# ACKNOWLEDGMENTS

Recipes
by Louis Pappas

Food stylist
Nancy Pappas

Photography & design
Charles Eanes

Editor
Susan Eanes

Copyright © 2002
by Louis & Nancy Pappas
All rights reserved. No part of this book may be reproduced in any form without the written permission from the publishers.

Library of Congress
Control Number 2002091731
ISBN 1-890494-07-0

Published by Espichel Enterprises
First Edition
Printed in the USA
by Marimark Corporation®

We wish to extend a special thanks to Alexander Pappas Gould, Coni Pappas, Florinda Pappas Williams, Aunt Pauline Melissas and Chef Petros Koulianos for their contributions and help in the production of this book.

Additional copies of "Louis Pappas New Generation Greek Cuisine" are available through major booksellers, on Amazon.com, at any Louis Pappas Market Cafe location or Louis Pappas' Riverside Restaurant. You may order by visiting our website at www.louispappas.com

# Contents

*Introduction...Page 4*

*Pappas History...Page 6*

*Louis Pappas...Page 7*

*Soups & Salads...8*

*Appetizers...20*

*Pastas...34*

*Seafood...42*

*Meats & Poultry...64*

*Traditional Greek..80*

*Breads & Desserts..94*

# INTRODUCTION

There is a vibrant beauty about Greece, from the surrounding azure seas to the vine covered mountains and the crisp white buildings that seem to stimulate all one's senses. It is also found in the warmth of the Greek people and their intimate love of life and their enjoyment of food.

Food in Greece provides more than nourishment. It is associated with music, gaiety, seasons and holidays, pervading every aspect of their culture as a way to link families and friends.

Greek recipes handed down from the early Bronze Age reached their pinnacle in the fifth century B.C. and were included in the earliest published books about cooking. This book pays tribute to many of those classic Greek dishes and to the family of Louis M. Pappamichalopoulos and their traditional recipes, which celebrate Greek cuisine in all its varieties.

The recipes by grandson Louis L. Pappas are a compilation of the best traditional dishes as well as updated versions that feature a "New Generation" of Greek cuisine. From the Louis Pappas Famous Greek Salad™ to Mama Pappas' Rice Pudding, all the tried and tested recipes of this book have made the landmark Louis Pappas' Riverside Restaurant a favorite of both locals and visitors for over 75 years.

## Louis M. Pappas with Mama, Michael, Lucas & Jack

# Pappas History

Louis M. Pappamichalopoulos came to America in 1904 from Sparta, Greece and for obvious reasons shortened his name to Pappas. During World War I he served in France as an army chef in General Pershing's "Wildcat Division". It was there he created his own version of a Greek salad by adding potato salad in order to sustain the troops during hard times.

In 1925, he and his wife Flora established the original "Riverside Cafe" in Tarpon Springs, with a handful of employees and sawdust floors. They specialized in fine Greek American cuisine and Louis Pappas' Greek salad. Potato salad at the bottom of a Greek salad became common place and the salad itself became internationally known.

With the assistance of their five children, Michael, Lucas, Jack, Bertha and Nina, the restaurant prospered over the years. Due to the tremendous popularity, the family opened several restaurants in the Tampa Bay area. They eventually combined their efforts under one roof in Tarpon Springs where Louis Pappas' Riverside Restaurant remains a landmark today. Through his many business ventures, grandson Louis Lucas Pappas remains committed to continuing over 75 years of Pappas tradition by providing the same high standard of quality and service set forth by the generations before him.

# Louis L. Pappas

After a lifetime in the business, third generation Louis Lucas Pappas remains committed to expanding the horizon of Greek cuisine while providing a modern and elegant dining experience for his clientele.

Without abandoning the heritage that inspired their menu, Louis has created a "New Generation" of Greek cuisine that puts a delightful twist on traditional dishes as we know them. He has searched the world for flavors that complement and marry well with the Greek Taste.

In keeping with the times Louis has expanded into the Tampa Bay area with his fast-casual concept under the name of Louis Pappas Market Cafe.℠ Staged in an old world marketplace setting, the Market Cafe chain caters to the busy lifestyle of today's consumer on the go.

Along with homemade soups, gourmet Mediterranean sandwiches and the world famous Louis Pappas Greek salad, the menu also provides an array of "prepared to order" meals to eat in or take out.

Louis also has his own private label extra virgin olive oil imported from Greece. This special oil, available in local markets and on his website, is derived purely from the first cold pressing of the Korineki variety olive commonly known as Kalamata. As with this fine oil used exclusively in his cooking, Louis selects only the highest quality ingredients to create the simplistic recipes in his "New Generation Greek Cuisine" cookbook.

# SOUPS & SALADS

## Chicken Egg Lemon Soup
### "Avgolemono Soupa"

 *Serves eight to ten*

*The Greek version of "Chicken Soup for the Soul", this traditional soup is thickened with a lemon and egg sauce called Avgolemono.*

### INGREDIENTS
1 large whole chicken
6 quarts water
3 tbsp chicken bouillon
2 cups orzo pasta
3 eggs
3/4 cup fresh lemon juice
salt & pepper to taste
cornstarch to thicken if needed
chopped parsley for garnish
lemon slices

### METHOD
*Wash and clean chicken. Place in a large pot and add water. Cover and bring to a hard boil for 20 minutes, then reduce to a medium boil for 45 minutes. Remove and skin and bone chicken. Pull meat into bite size pieces and set aside. To stock, add bouillon and bring to a medium boil. Add the orzo and cook uncovered, stirring continuously for approximately 30 minutes. Remove from heat.*

*In a separate bowl, beat eggs while adding lemon juice. Slowly add 6 ladles of chicken stock, continually beating to avoid curdling. Pour mixture back into original stock. Add chicken and salt and pepper to taste. Serve garnished with lemon slices and chopped parsley.*

## Avgolemono Soupa

# SOUPS & SALADS

## Tomato Orzo Soup

 Serves eight to ten

As long as there was a shell, hollowed stone or a pot the Greeks have made soups. This soup is the foundation for many others. Use your imagination and experiment. Add fresh white fish or lamb. The longer it simmers the better the taste.

### INGREDIENTS
2-1/2 cups orzo pasta
1/4 lb butter
1-1/2 cups chopped onion
1 heaping tbsp chopped garlic
3 tsp salt
2 tsp pepper
1 tsp dried Greek oregano
2 cups chopped & seeded tomatoes
3 cups crushed canned tomatoes
1/2 cup tomato paste
1/4 tsp crushed red pepper
4 large basil leaves, chopped
3 quarts cold water

### METHOD
In a stock pot saute onions, garlic, salt, pepper and oregano in melted butter over medium heat until onions are clear. Add fresh tomatoes, canned tomatoes, tomato paste and crushed red pepper and simmer for 15 minutes. Add water, increase heat, cover and bring to a boil. Add orzo and cook uncovered, stirring continuously until fully cooked. Reduce heat, simmer for additional 30 minutes then add basil. Remove from heat and garnish with basil leaves to serve.

# Tomato Orzo Soup

# SOUPS & SALADS

## Louis Pappas Famous Greek Salad ™

*This is the original 1925 salad with the potato salad at the bottom that made "Riverside Cafe" known worldwide.*

 Serves four

**Greek Salad**

2 medium heads of iceberg lettuce
4 cups potato salad (above)
2 tomatoes cut into 4 wedges each
1 cucumber peeled & cut lengthwise into 4 fingers or wedges
1 avocado peeled & cut into wedges
4 radishes
8 Kalamata olives
8 Salonika peppers
4 large leaves curly spinach
2 feta slices, 4 oz each, 1/4" thick
4 green bell pepper rings, 1/4" thick
4 beet slices
4 shrimp cooked and peeled
4 anchovy fillets
4 whole scallions
1 cup Pappas' extra virgin olive oil
1 cup distilled white vinegar
2 tsp dried Greek oregano

**Potato Salad**

5 lbs boiled potatoes, peeled & diced
2 cups finely chopped onions
1/2 cup finely chopped green bell pepper
1 cup finely chopped scallions
3 cups mayonnaise
3 tsp salt
Mix all ingredients to prepare salad

**Method**

Line a large platter with the outside lettuce leaves, creating a shell. Place the potato salad in the center. Slice the lettuce heads into 1/8" cross cuts. Shape lettuce into a pyramid over the potato salad. At the base of the lettuce, alternate cucumber and tomato wedges. Continue around the base of the pyramid arranging the radishes, Salonika peppers, avocado wedges and olives. Place the spinach leaves on top of the pyramid followed by the feta cheese slices. Lay the pepper rings on the cheese and place the beet slices inside the rings. At the top place a shrimp on each beet slice and lay an anchovy fillet on each shrimp. Arrange the scallions with the tops standing up around the salad. Sprinkle finished salad with olive oil, vinegar and oregano.

# Louis Pappas Famous Greek Salad ™

13

# SOUPS & SALADS

## Village Salad
### "Horiatiki Salata"

 *Serves six to ten*

*In Greece, horio means "village" and this salad, unrefined and filled with large cut chunks of vegetables, is typical of country fare.*

**INGREDIENTS**
2 large cucumbers
2 green bell peppers
4 scallions
1 lb feta cheese
20 Salonika peppers (pepperoncini)
30 jumbo Kalamata olives
10 large radishes
1 cup sliced cooked beets
1-1/2 cups garbanzo beans,
    cooked & drained
4 medium firm tomatoes
1 large sweet onion

*For dressing*
3/4 cup fresh lemon juice, strained
1-1/2 cups Pappas' extra virgin olive oil
2 tbsp dried Greek oregano
1/2 cup red wine vinegar
1 tbsp salt
1 tbsp black pepper
1 tsp finely chopped fresh garlic

**METHOD**
Quarter cucumbers lengthwise and cut into 1/2" slices. Cut bell peppers into 1/2" squares and the scallions into 1" lengths. Hand crumble feta into large chunks. Cut radishes in half and julienne the beets. Cut each tomato into 8 wedges and the onion into 1" chunks. In a large bowl lightly toss all of these ingredients together with Salonika peppers, olives and garbanzo beans until well mixed.

*Method for dressing*
Whisk all ingredients together until well mixed, pour over salad and serve immediately.

## Horiatiki Salata

# SOUPS & SALADS

## Bahamian Conch Salad

 *Serves six*

*A close second to the Greek Isles, the Bahamas have been a vacation destination of the Pappas family for years. Discovered in the Abacos, this recipe has become a family favorite.*

### INGREDIENTS
*1 lb very clean conch, dark skin removed*
*1 cup finely chopped celery (tender stems)*
*3/4 cup finely chopped onion*
*1 tbsp finely chopped red pepper*
*1 tbsp finely chopped yellow pepper*
*3/4 cup Pappas' extra virgin olive oil*
*1/2 cup freshly squeezed lemon juice*
*1/4 cup freshly squeezed lime juice*
*1/2 tsp coarse black pepper*
*1/2 tsp salt*
*1/2 small bird pepper, chopped (optional)*
*chopped mango (optional)*

### METHOD
*Finely chop conch and place in a bowl with celery, onions and bell peppers. Pour olive oil, lemon and lime juice over. Season to taste and blend all together. Marinate for at least 30 minutes to allow flavors to blend. Salad will hold in refrigerator for 3 or 4 days. Garnish with parsley and serve with toast rounds.*
*In lieu of the red pepper, you can use a bird pepper, but only use half of a small one because they are very hot. Including some chopped fresh mango makes this salad a little less tangy and a lot more colorful.*

# Bahamian Conch Salad

# SOUPS & SALADS

## Greek Pasta Salad

 Serves six

Inspired by Louie's sister, Florinda, this salad is great alone or served as we do, with one of our great sandwiches.

### INGREDIENTS
1 lb white or tri-colored twist pasta
1 large tomato
1 cucumber
1/2 lb feta cheese
3/4 cup pimento stuffed green olives

### For dressing
3/4 cup salad oil
1/4 cup white vinegar
1/4 cup seasoned rice vinegar
pinch dried dill weed
pinch fresh chopped parsley
pinch black pepper
pinch dried basil

### METHOD
Cook pasta until al dente and drain well. Dice the tomato and add to pasta along with the cucumber, peeled and diced. Crumble the feta over pasta and add olives. Toss well with dressing and serve chilled.

### Method for dressing
Combine all ingredients and blend well. Be sure not to add any salt.

# Greek Pasta Salad

# APPETIZERS

## Bruschetta with Crumbled Feta Cheese

 Serves four

Married to an Italian, Louie often infuses Italian into his cooking. Feta, a fresh white curd cheese, was originally made from sheep's or goat's milk. Today it is more commonly made from cow's milk.

### INGREDIENTS
2 cups chopped seeded tomatoes
1/4 cup chopped sweet basil
1/2 cup finely chopped onion
1 tsp minced garlic
1 pinch crushed red pepper
1/4 tsp salt
1 tbsp lemon juice
1/2 tbsp red wine vinegar
2 tbsp Pappas' extra virgin olive oil

### METHOD
Seed tomatoes and chop into 1/4" pieces. Combine with remaining ingredients and mix well. Put Bruschetta mixture in bowl and surround with toast points. Sprinkle with feta cheese.

# Bruschetta

# APPETIZERS

## Marinated Octopus

 Serves two

*This favorite Mediterranean way of preparing octopus is called "oktapodi tursi" in Greece.*

### INGREDIENTS
2 cleaned octopi, 2 lbs each
1 cup dry red wine
2 oz pickling spice
water
1/2 cup chopped tomatoes
1/2 cup chopped onions

### For marinade
1 cup white vinegar
1/2 cup fresh lemon juice
2 cups Pappas' extra virgin olive oil
1 heaping tbsp chopped fresh garlic
1 heaping tbsp dried Greek oregano
pinch of crushed red pepper
3 bay leaves
1 tsp salt

### METHOD
Cover octopus with water in a boiling pot. Add red wine and pickling spice. Cover and boil for approximately 45 minutes or until tender. Remove from pot and rinse in cold running water. Separate each tentacle and, if desired, cut into 2" pieces. Add to marinade and refrigerate for at least two hours. Remove from marinade, arrange on plate and top with onions and tomatoes.

### Method for marinade
Whisk all ingredients together until well combined. Salt to taste. For a milder marinade, add more olive oil or a splash of water.

# Marinated Octopus

# APPETIZERS

## Flaming Cheese
### "Saganaki"

 Serves two

**INGREDIENTS**
5 oz Kefalotyri
3 tbsp flour
1/4 cup blended oil
1 cup milk
1 egg
1/2 lemon
1 tsp chopped parsley
1 oz Metaxa 5-star brandy
  (or any 151 proof brandy)

While many cheeses are now mass produced, Greek cheeses remain straight forward and authentic, made the old fashion way. Kefalotyri is a hard Greek, aged cheese made from goat's milk commonly used for grating, but sliced here to make Saganaki.

**METHOD**
Slice the Kefalotyri into 4" squares, 1/4" thick. Mix egg and milk together well. Dip cheese slices into batter and then into flour. Heat blended oil in a serving dish or 8 inch metal pan until very hot. Add cheese and cook to a golden brown on each side. Strain off oil. Add brandy and flame, and say "Opah"! Douse flame by squeezing lemon and garnish with parsley.
Serve immediately.

# Saganaki

# APPETIZERS

## Mediterranean Spreads

 *Makes eight servings each*

These spreads may be served with crostinis, crackers or grilled pita bread, individually or all together on one platter.

### Kalamata Olive
7 oz pitted Kalamata olives, drained
4 oz feta cheese
8 oz cream cheese, softened
8 oz sour cream
2 tsp dried dill

**Method for Olive**
Place olives in food processor and blend with feta, cream cheese and sour cream. Add dill and blend until smooth.

### Roasted Eggplant "Melitzanosalata"
3 medium size eggplants, peeled
10 large garlic cloves, peeled
2 tbsp fresh lemon juice
3 tbsp Pappas' extra virgin olive oil
1/4 tsp crushed red pepper
1/4 tsp salt

**Method for Eggplant**
Cut eggplant into 1/8" slices, salt and let stand for 30 minutes. Rinse, dip in oil and place on greased pan with garlic. Bake on high heat until edges are brown and crispy and garlic is tender. Coarsely chop eggplant and garlic and mix with remaining ingredients.

### Hummus
3 cups dried garbanzo beans
2/3 cup chopped roasted eggplant
2-1/2 cups Pappas' extra virgin olive oil
1 heaping tbsp fresh chopped garlic
4 tbsp lemon juice
3/4 tsp coarse black pepper
1 tsp salt

**Method for Hummus**
Cover beans with water, add salt and bring to a boil. Cook, keeping beans covered with water, for about 1 hour until beans are al dente. Drain and reserve water. Process beans in a blender with 1-1/2 cups of reserved water. Add remaining ingredients and blend until very smooth.

# Mediterranean Spreads

# APPETIZERS

## Caribbean Grouper Wraps

 Serves four

*Another culinary treasure found around the turquoise waters of the Bahamas, this one was worth bringing home.*

### INGREDIENTS
1 lb fresh Florida black grouper
8 oz can sliced water chestnuts
16 slices of thin sliced bacon

### For marinade
1-1/2 cups water
3/4 cup Teriyaki sauce
1/4 cup sesame oil
2 tbsp yellow mustard
1/4 cup lemon juice
1 tbsp chopped garlic
2 tbsp chopped Italian parsley
1 tbsp dried Greek oregano

### METHOD
Cut grouper into one ounce pieces. Cut bacon strips in half and lay in a row on counter. Place one water chestnut slice on one end, top with a grouper chunk, followed by another water chestnut slice on top of grouper. Repeat procedure for each bacon strip. Carefully roll the bacon with ingredients inside and secure with a toothpick. Blend all marinade ingredients and pour over grouper wraps to coat well. Cover and chill for two hours to infuse flavors. Charbroil or bake over medium heat until the bacon is well done and the fish is thoroughly cooked. Drain on paper towels and serve while hot and crispy.

# Caribbean Grouper Wraps

29

# APPETIZERS

## Fried Eggplant & Zucchini with Skordalia

 Serves six

### INGREDIENTS
2 large zucchini
1 medium eggplant
2 eggs
2 cups milk
3 cups flour
3 tbsp salt
3/4 tbsp pepper
3/4 cup Pappas' extra virgin olive oil
3/4 cup melted butter
4 oz grated cheese
chopped parsley for garnish

### For Skordalia
3 large potatoes, boiled to tenderness
2 cups Pappas' extra virgin olive oil
3/4 cup finely chopped garlic
1/4 cup red wine vinegar
1/4 cup mayonnaise
1 tsp each salt & black pepper

*In Greece anything that has been deep fried is drained on newspapers, rather than on paper towels. A garlic lover's delight, Skordalia is a potato based spread served with many dishes or as a dip for fried vegetables.*

### METHOD
Cut zucchini into rounds 1/4" thick. Cut eggplant into 2" squares, 1/4" thick. Salt, let stand 30 minutes and rinse. Dip zucchini and eggplant into egg and milk batter. Dredge in flour seasoned with salt and pepper. In a large skillet heat oil and butter until hot. Pan fry vegetables until golden brown on both sides and done inside. Drain off oil on newspapers. Place Skordalia in the middle of a plate and surround with zucchini and eggplant. Sprinkle with cheese and parsley.

### Method for Skordalia
In a food processor blend olive oil and garlic. While processing add vinegar, mayonnaise, salt and pepper. Add potatoes after removing their skins and blend to paste texture.

# Fried Eggplant & Zucchini

# APPETIZERS

## Spanakopita & Tiropita with Tzatziki Sauce

**INGREDIENTS For Spanakopita**
1 lb fresh spinach, chopped
4 tbsp Pappas' extra virgin olive oil
2 cups chopped leeks
1 cup chopped scallions
2 tbsp dried dill, 1 egg, 1 tsp salt
3 cups feta cheese, crumbled
1 cup cottage cheese
1/2 cup grated Romano cheese
1 lb phyllo dough

**INGREDIENTS For Tiropita**
2 cups crumbled feta cheese
1 cup cottage cheese
1 cup grated Romano cheese
1 egg
1 tsp dried sweet basil
1/2 lb phyllo dough

**INGREDIENTS For Tzatziki Sauce**
1 cucumber, seeded and grated
1 cup plain yogurt
1/4 cup chopped fresh parsley
1 heaping tbsp finely chopped garlic
1 tbsp Pappas' extra virgin olive oil
2 tbsp fresh lemon juice, 1 tsp salt

Of Greek origin, a tablespoon of these fillings is placed onto a buttered phyllo sheet folded 4" wide, then folded like a flag into triangle shaped pies and baked for 40 minutes at 350° until golden.

**METHOD for Spanakopita**
In a large pot, saute leeks, scallions and dill in oil over medium heat for 3 to 4 minutes until soft. Add spinach, mix well and cook an additional 5 minutes until spinach is wilted. Remove from heat and add remaining ingredients. Mix well. Makes filling for ten to twelve triangles.

**METHOD for Tiropita**
Mix all ingredients together by hand until well blended.
Makes filling for six triangles.

**METHOD for Tzatziki Sauce**
In a food processor blend parsley, garlic, oil, lemon juice and salt until smooth. Remove from processor and mix well with cucumber and yogurt. Place in small bowl beside triangle pies for dipping.
Makes six servings.

# Spanakopita & Tiropita

# PASTAS

## Seafood Pasta

 Serves two

*This particular dish has a very clean flavor, focusing on enjoying fresh seafood along with your pasta.*

### INGREDIENTS
6 large shrimp, peeled & deveined
6 New Zealand mussels
6 large sea scallops
10 small middleneck clams
1 cup water
1/3 cup Pappas' extra virgin olive oil
1 oz butter
1/2 small white onion, chopped
1-1/2 tbsp chopped garlic
1/4 tsp crushed red pepper
1 tbsp chopped parsley
3/4 cup white wine
2 large basil leaves, chopped fine
2 tbsp grated Romano cheese
salt & pepper to taste
1 lb linguine, cooked al dente

### METHOD
Steam clams in water in covered pan until they are slightly opened. Remove from heat and set aside, leaving clams in the water. In a saute pan, heat butter and oil and add onion, garlic, red pepper and parsley. After onions are clear, add white wine. Add shrimp first, mussels second, scallops and the basil. Then add the clams along with the water used for steaming. Salt and pepper to taste, cover and simmer until all shellfish are open, approximately 3 to 5 minutes. Place pasta on plate and arrange seafood evenly on top. Sprinkle with grated Romano and chopped parsley.

# Seafood Pasta

# PASTAS

## Halkitika Macaronia

 Serves two

Originated on the island of Halki, this pasta is prepared with Mizithra cheese. Mizithra is a whey cheese that is low in fat, worth searching for. Italian ricotta, however, is a very close substitute.

**INGREDIENTS**
1 large onion, chopped
6 oz melted butter
salt & pepper to taste
1 tsp chopped garlic
1 tbsp chopped parsley
1/4 cup grated Mizithra cheese
1/4 cup grated Kaseri cheese
1/4 cup grated Romano cheese
1 lb linguine, cooked al dente

**METHOD**
Over high heat, bring 4 ounces of butter to smoking stage. Add onion, salt and pepper and cook, while tossing, until onions are dark golden brown. Add garlic, remaining butter, parsley and toss. Add pasta, toss and remove from heat. Add mixture of three cheeses, saving small amount for garnish, and toss well again. Mound pasta and onion cheese mixture on plates and sprinkle with remaining cheese mixture. Serve immediately.

# Halkitika Macaronia

# PASTAS

## Shrimp & Feta Pasta

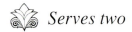 Serves two

A Pappas favorite. Large shrimp are sauteed with fresh tomato, parsley and garlic blended with crumbled feta and served over pasta.

### INGREDIENTS
12 large shrimp
2 tbsp flour
1/4 cup Pappas' extra virgin olive oil
1 oz melted butter
1/3 cup white wine
1 tsp chopped garlic
3/4 cup diced tomatoes
1/4 tsp crushed red pepper
pinch of salt
pinch of dried Greek oregano
1 cup marinara sauce (see page 76)
1 tbsp chopped parsley
3 oz feta cheese, crumbled
grated Romano or Mizithra (optional)
1 lb linquine, cooked al dente

### METHOD
Peel and devein shrimp and lightly flour. Over medium fire, heat butter and oil and add shrimp. Cook until light brown on one side and then turn. Drain excess oil and return to medium heat. Add white wine and flame. When flame diminishes, add garlic, tomatoes, red pepper, salt and oregano. Add marinara sauce and simmer for 3 minutes. Remove from heat, add feta and parsley and mix well. Mound pasta on plate and pour sauce over. Garnish with chopped parsley and top with grated Romano or Mizithra if desired.

# Shrimp & Feta Pasta

# PASTAS

## Clams Chardonnay with Sun Dried Tomato Cream Sauce

 *Serves four*

*This simple dish is a reduction of quality wine, fresh clam juice, chopped sweet onions and heavy cream.*

### INGREDIENTS
25 littleneck clams
1 cup chopped clams
1/4 cup Pappas' extra virgin olive oil
3 oz butter
1-1/2 cups chopped onion
2 tsp sea salt
1 tsp white pepper
2 cups Chardonnay wine
1-1/2 cups clam juice
2 tbsp finely chopped garlic
4 tbsp finely chopped Italian parsley
2 tbsp chopped fresh basil
1/4 cup chopped sun dried tomatoes
1/2 cup heavy cream
1/2 cup grated Romano cheese
1-1/2 lb linguine, cooked al dente

### METHOD
In a saute pan, heat butter and oil and add onions, salt and white pepper. When onions start to clear, add wine and clam juice. Cook over high heat and reduce by 2/3. Once sauce has been reduced, add garlic, parsley and basil. Reduce to medium heat and add the whole clams. If sauce seems too thick, add 1/2 cup water. Cover and cook until clams begin to open. Add chopped clams, sun dried tomatoes, heavy cream and Romano cheese. Simmer 3 to 5 minutes until sauce is of a light syrup consistency. Place pasta on plates and cover with sauce, evenly dividing the seafood. Sprinkle with chopped parsley.

# Clams Chardonnay

# SEAFOOD

## Butter Pan Fried & "Old Style" U-Peel' Em Shrimp

These simple, but delicious, shrimp dishes are best with fresh Florida Gulf Coast shrimp, preferably whites or pinks.

 *Each serves four*

**INGREDIENTS for Pan Fried Shrimp**
2 lbs large shrimp (16 count)
salt & pepper to taste
1 cup flour
1/4 cup Pappas' extra virgin olive oil
2 tbsp butter
1 lemon

**METHOD for Pan Fried Shrimp**
*Peel and devein shrimp. Rinse well under cold water. Drain and sprinkle lightly with salt and pepper. Dredge in flour and shake off excess. Heat oil and butter in large skillet until very hot, add shrimp and cook until lightly browned on both sides, taking care not to overcook. Squeeze lemon juice over and serve.*

**INGREDIENTS for U-Peel' Em Shrimp**
2 lbs large shrimp (16 count)
Pappas' extra virgin olive oil for grilling
salt & pepper to taste
Greek Style sauce (see page 48)
crumbled feta cheese
chopped parsley
Salonika peppers (pepperoncini)

**METHOD for U-Peel' Em Shrimp**
*Salt and pepper shrimp. On hot grill sprinkled with olive oil, cook shrimp until pink on both sides, careful not to overcook. Plate shrimp and sprinkle with Greek Style sauce. Top with feta, parsley and Salonika peppers.*

# Pan Fried & U-Peel' Em Shrimp

# SEAFOOD

## Fire Grilled Florida Whole Red Snapper
### With Skewered Fresh Vegetables

 *Serves four to five*

*This one is great for outdoor grilling. Make sure the grill is well oiled to prevent sticking.*

### INGREDIENTS
2 Florida whole red snappers, 2-1/2 lbs each
3 cups Greek Style sauce (see page 48)

2 pear tomatoes
2 zucchini
1 green bell pepper
1 red bell pepper
1 yellow bell pepper
2 red onions
salt & pepper to taste

### METHOD
Clean, scale and gill fish. Score sides with a sharp knife 1/4" deep and approximately 1-1/2" apart. Sprinkle fish thoroughly with Greek Style sauce on inside and out. Salt and pepper fish, rubbing into slits. Place fish on medium heat on well oiled char broiler and cover to keep from drying. When edges of fish turn white (approximately 15 minutes), flip over and grill opposite side for another 15 minutes. Baste with Greek Style sauce during the cooking process.

Coarsely cut tomatoes, zucchini, peppers and onions and place on skewers for grilling. During last few minutes of cooking fish, place vegetable skewers on grill and baste with Greek Style sauce as well. Plate fish on a serving platter and surround with the grilled vegetables.

# Grilled Red Snapper

# SEAFOOD

## Pan Fried Bahamian Cracked Conch

 *Serves four*

Ask your local fish market for shallow water Caribbean conch that has been completely skinned to ensure a tender texture.

**INGREDIENTS**
1-1/2 lbs cleaned conch
2 eggs
1/2 cup milk
salt & pepper to taste
2 cups flour
1/2 cup Pappas' extra virgin olive oil
5 oz butter
1 tbsp dried Greek oregano
1 tbsp chopped parsley
4 lemon wedges

**METHOD**
Cut conch into medallions, 4 ounces to 6 ounces each. Place medallions on a chopping block and pound with a mallet for tenderness. Beat eggs and milk together. Dip conch into egg mixture, salt and pepper to taste, then lightly dredge in flour. Heat oil and butter in skillet until very hot. Place medallions in the pan and cook until lightly golden brown on both sides. Remove from the pan and arrange on plates. Sprinkle lightly with Greek oregano and parsley. Serve with lemon wedges.

# Bahamian Cracked Conch

# SEAFOOD

## Grilled Black Grouper with Greek Style Sauce

 *Serves four*

*Louie will only buy the freshest Florida black grouper caught in local waters of the Gulf of Mexico.*

### INGREDIENTS
4 Florida black grouper 8 oz fillets
Pappas' extra virgin olive oil
salt & pepper to taste
4 tomato wedges
4 lemon twists
Kalamata olives

### For Greek Style sauce
1 cup Pappas' extra virgin olive oil
2/3 cup fresh lemon juice
2 tbsp fresh chopped garlic
1-1/2 tbsp dried Greek oregano
1/2 cup chopped Italian parsley
1 tsp salt
1/2 tsp crushed red pepper

### METHOD
Season fish fillets and coat with olive oil. Char grill on both sides until cooked golden brown and moist in center, keeping covered if necessary. Place on a serving plate and garnish with lemon twists, tomato wedges and Kalamata olives. Douse fillets with well shaken Greek style sauce.

### Method for Greek sauce
In a large bowl, incorporate all ingredients and blend well.

# Grilled Grouper Greek Style

# SEAFOOD

## Grouper Aegean

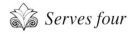 *Serves four*

### INGREDIENTS
4 grouper fillets, 8 oz each
10 oz feta cheese, crumbled
3/4 cup finely chopped Italian parsley
2-1/2 cups diced & seeded firm tomatoes
3/4 cup dry white wine
3 tsp finely chopped garlic
1 tsp salt
2 tsp fresh ground black pepper
lemon slices & tomato wedges for garnish

### For rice pilaf
2 quarts water
2 cups uncooked rice
2 cups butter
1 cup chopped onions
1 cup chopped pimento
1 cup chicken stock

*The "Aegean" mixture is served as a warm salad topping for fish. It is also great alone as a cold salad.*

### METHOD
*Cook fillets on lightly oiled flat grill until golden on both sides. Mix remaining Aegean ingredients well by hand. Place fish on broiler pan and top with liberal amount of Aegean mixture. Place under broiler to warm topping, approximately 1 minute. Arrange on plates and serve with rice pilaf. Garnish with lemon slices and tomato wedges.*

### Method for rice pilaf
*Bring water, butter and onions to a boil. Add chicken stock and bring to a boil again. Add rice and pimento, reduce to medium heat and cook until water is absorbed, about 20 minutes. Cover and let stand for four to five minutes.*

# Grouper Aegean

# SEAFOOD

## Pan Seared Sea Scallops with Greek Yogurt Sauce

 *Serves three to four*

### INGREDIENTS
2 lbs large sea scallops
3/4 cup Pappas' extra virgin olive oil
2 cups flour
chopped parsley for garnish

### For Greek yogurt sauce
1 large red or yellow bell pepper
3/4 cup coarsely chopped Italian parsley
1/2 cup fresh lemon juice
1/2 tsp crushed red pepper flakes
1 heaping tbsp coarsely chopped garlic
2 tsp sea salt
1-1/2 cups plain yogurt
1 tbsp red wine vinegar
1 cup Pappas' extra virgin olive oil
1/2 tsp black pepper

*In most every Greek village you will find yogurt hanging in linen bags to drain off the liquid. Louie uses only homemade yogurt, but the commercial variety is fine for this recipe.*

### METHOD
*In large frying pan heat oil until smoking hot. Lightly dredge scallops in flour and place one half in pan. Sear the scallops to a golden brown on each side. Sear the other half the same. Remove pan from heat and drain off oil. Add 1-1/2 cups of yogurt sauce to hot pan and swirl with all scallops to infuse flavors. Arrange scallops on plates and pour additional sauce over if desired. Garnish with chopped parsley.*

### Method for Greek yogurt sauce
*Rub pepper with oil and rotate on charbroiler until roasted and soft and semi-burnt in color. Remove stems and seeds, coarsely chop and add to all remaining ingredients in a blender. Blend until smooth.*

# Seared Sea Scallops

# SEAFOOD

## Charbroiled Octopus

 *Serves two*

### INGREDIENTS
2 octopi, 2 lbs each, cleaned & tenderized
1 cup dry red wine
2 oz pickling spice
water
10 Kalamata olives
2 oz feta cheese, cubed
tomato wedges
1 tbsp chopped parsley

### For vinaigrette
1/4 cup fresh lemon juice
1/4 cup balsamic vinegar
1/2 cup red wine vinegar
3 cups Pappas' extra virgin olive oil
4 garlic cloves, finely chopped
3 tsp dried Greek oregano
1 tsp salt
1 tsp coarse ground black pepper

*In Greece octopus is prepared a dozen ways and can even taste like lobster. Try this method and you will agree.*

### METHOD
Cover octopus with water in a boiling pot. Add red wine and pickling spice. Boil covered for approximately 45 minutes or until tender. Remove from pot and rinse in cold running water. Separate each tentacle. Place on a charbroiler and baste with vinaigrette while cooking on both sides until crispy and done. Arrange octopus on plates and top with olives and feta cheese. Dress with the vinaigrette, add tomato wedges and sprinkle with parsley.

### Method for vinaigrette
Combine all ingredients in bowl and whisk until well blended. (Left over vinaigrette should be refrigerated).

# Charbroiled Octopus

# SEAFOOD

## 3rd Generation Grouper

 *Serves four*

This dish features a marinade of lemon, garlic and mustard sauce designed by Louie, a 3rd generation Pappas.

### INGREDIENTS
4 fresh Florida grouper 8 oz fillets
3 oz melted butter
6 oz Pappas' extra virgin olive oil
3 cups flour
salt & pepper to taste
4 lemon slices
chopped parsley for garnish
4 cups Skordalia (see page 30)

### For marinade
1/4 cup chopped garlic
2 tbsp Worcestershire sauce
1 tbsp salt
2 cups lemon juice
1 cup mustard
1 tbsp black pepper

### METHOD
Mix all marinade ingredients together well. Refrigerate fillets in marinade for approximately 4 hours. Remove grouper from marinade. Salt and pepper and lightly dredge in flour. Place fillets in mixture of hot oil and butter. In a skillet, cook over medium heat on one side until golden brown, being careful not to burn. Turn and brown other side to golden. Plate grouper and garnish with lemon slices and parsley. Serve with Skordalia over sauteed spinach.

# 3rd Generation Grouper

# SEAFOOD

## Salmon Spanaki

 Serves six

*Use fresh Chilean farm raised salmon to stuff with this spinach mixture, the same used in Spanakopita pastry.*

### INGREDIENTS
6 salmon fillets, 8 oz each
salt & pepper to taste
3 oz butter, softened
2 tsp paprika
2 tbsp chopped parsley
6 lemon wedges
4 oz lemon herb butter

### For spinach stuffing
1 lb fresh spinach, chopped
4 tbsp Pappas' extra virgin olive oil
2 cups chopped leeks
1 cup chopped scallions
2 tbsp dried dill
3 cups feta cheese, crumbled
1 cup cottage cheese
1/2 cup grated Romano cheese
1 egg
1 tsp salt

### METHOD
Remove skin and bones from salmon and make an incision lengthwise down the middle of each fillet as if to butterfly. Salt and pepper to taste. Stuff each fillet with approximately one cup of spinach mixture. Press fillets closed to a 1" gap. Place salmon in a roasting pan with water covering the bottom. Sprinkle with paprika and top each fillet with 1/2 oz butter. Cook in 350° oven for approximately 15 minutes until cooked through but not dry, covering with foil if necessary. Place fillets on plates and top each with a dollop of butter blended with lemon juice and herbs. Garnish with lemon wedges and chopped parsley.

### Method for spinach stuffing
In a large pot, saute leeks, scallions and dill in oil over medium heat. Add spinach and cook until wilted. Remove from heat and add remaining ingredients. Mix well and cool.

# Salmon Spanaki

# SEAFOOD

## Peppered Shrimp

 Serves two

*Served for years in the restaurant, this Peppered Shrimp recipe is a treasured gift from the late Art Pepin, owner of Tampa's Anheuser Busch distributorship.*

### INGREDIENTS
16 to 20 large shrimp in shell (20 count)
1/4 cup Pappas' extra virgin olive oil
1 tbsp chopped garlic
2 lemon slices
4 lime slices
1/4 cup fresh lemon juice
3/4 tsp salt
1-1/2 tsp pepper
3 oz dry vermouth
chopped parsley for garnish

### METHOD
Heat oil in frying pan until hot and add shrimp. Cook on one side until pink, approximately 1 minute. Add garlic and reduce to medium heat and saute until shrimp are pink on one side. Turn shrimp, add lemon and lime slices, lemon juice, salt and pepper. Blend well and continue to saute over medium heat until done, taking care not to overcook shrimp. Add vermouth and cook for another 45 seconds until alcohol is cooked off. Adjust seasoning if necessary. Arrange lemon and lime slices on plate and surround with shrimp. Pour remaining pan juices over and garnish with chopped parsley.

# Peppered Shrimp

# SEAFOOD

## Butter Pan Fried Baby Squid
### "Kalamarakia"

 *Serves three*

**INGREDIENTS**
15 to 20 baby squid,
   3" to 4" long, uncleaned
3/4 cup Pappas' extra virgin olive oil
3/4 cup melted butter
2 cups flour
1 tbsp dried Greek oregano
fresh lemon juice
3 scallions
3 tomato wedges
1 cup red vegetable sauce (see page 111)
3 cups rice pilaf (see page 50)

It is important to purchase whole baby Pacific squid. The best ones come from Monterey.

**METHOD**
Under cold running water remove beak, ink sack and inner tube and clean squid thoroughly leaving outer skin on. Cut the head (tentacles) from the body. In a large frying pan heat mixture of butter and oil until very hot. Lightly dredge squid in flour and place in the frying pan one at a time, body first, then tentacles. Butter and oil mixture should cover 1/4 of side of squid. Fry crisp on one side and turn delicately. When almost done, carefully drain off oil mixture and return to high heat for 1 minute more to ensure crispiness. Arrange squid on a plate around a mound of rice pilaf. Top rice with red vegetable sauce and sprinkle with lemon juice and oregano. Garnish with scallions and tomato wedges.

# Kalamarakia

# MEATS & POULTRY

## Roast Leg of Lamb
### "Arni Sto Fourno"

 *Serves ten to twelve*

### INGREDIENTS
10 lb leg of lamb, bone in & trimmed
1 cup Greek Style sauce  (see page 48)
1-1/2 tbsp salt
1 tbsp black pepper
2 heaping tbsp dried Greek oregano
1/2 cup chopped garlic
3 cups water
Brown lamb sauce  (see page 110)

### For Greek Style oven brown potatoes
5 baking potatoes
1/4 cup dried Greek oregano
1/2 cup chopped garlic
1 lb ground lamb trimmings
1/2 cup fresh lemon juice
1-1/2 cups water
1/2 cup melted butter
salt & pepper to taste

*Easter is the most celebrated religious event in Greece.  Lamb is the traditional fare, served with hard boiled eggs dyed red.*

### METHOD
Have your butcher grind lamb trimmings for use on potatoes.  Sprinkle lamb with Greek Style sauce.  Rub and coat lamb well with mixture of salt, pepper and oregano and then rub with garlic.  Let stand for 20 minutes at room temperature.  Place in roasting pan with water in the bottom and roast in 375° oven for 3 to 3-1/2 hours, basting with the drippings as it cooks.  After 1-1/2 hours, turn over.  Add more water if needed.  Using a thermometer, cook to an internal temperature of 170° for medium to medium well.  Place leg on carving platter and surround with potatoes.  Slice very thin and serve with brown lamb sauce.

### Method for potatoes
Quarter potatoes, place in a roasting pan and sprinkle with garlic, lamb trimmings, salt, pepper and oregano.  Mix lemon juice, water and butter and pour over potatoes.  Bake in 400° oven for approximately 40 minutes until potatoes are soft inside and browned on the outside.

# Arni Sto Fourno

# MEATS & POULTRY

## Prime Rib with Shoe String Onion Rings

 *Serves ten to twelve*

### INGREDIENTS
12 to 15 lb prime rib, bone in
2 cups Greek Style sauce  (see page 48)
1/2 cup salt
1/4 cup coarse black pepper
1/4 cup dried Greek oregano
3 cups water
5 to 6 cups brown beef sauce  (see page 110)

### For shoe string onion rings
3 large yellow onions
2 cups flour
2 tsp salt
1 tsp black pepper
1 cup blended oil for frying

*Known for its size and outstanding flavor, people drive from miles away just to enjoy Louie's Prime Rib.  The crispy onion rings make the perfect accompaniment.*

### METHOD
Pour Greek Style sauce over rib, rub well and season with a blend of salt, pepper and oregano.  Place water in bottom of roasting pan and place rib in pan.  In a 450° oven brown rib for 20 minutes.  Reduce heat to 325° and cook for about 1 hour and 15 minutes on each side, basting with juices and adding more water to pan if necessary.  Remove when cooked to desired doneness, preferably rare or 140° in center.  Note that the slower you cook the roast, the more tender it will be.  Serve with brown beef sauce and crispy shoe string onion rings.

### Method for onion rings
Cut the onions crosswise into very, very thin slices.  Break slices into rings and dip in flour seasoned with salt and pepper.  Shake off excess flour.  Heat oil in stock pot until very hot.  Quickly fry onions, small portions at a time, until golden brown.  Remove from oil, drain and serve with the prime rib.

# Prime Rib

# MEATS & POULTRY

## Roasted Pork with Fresh Yams

 *Serves eight to ten*

### INGREDIENTS
7 lb center cut pork loin, trimmed
1 cup Greek Style sauce  (see page 48)
1-1/2 tbsp salt
1-1/2 tbsp coarse black pepper
1-1/2 tbsp dried Greek oregano
1/2 tbsp dried whole thyme
3 cups water

### Ingredients for fresh yams
5 to 6 large yams
8 cups water
1 tsp salt
10 whole cloves
4 cups sugar
zest of 2 small oranges
2 cinnamon sticks, 2" long
1 lemon slice, 1/4" wide
1/2 lb butter
1 tbsp vanilla extract
1 tbsp ground cinnamon
1/2 cup walnuts

*Served only on Sundays and holidays, Papou Louie's roasted pork dates back to the days of sawdust floors at the Riverside Cafe.*

### METHOD
*Place loin in a roasting pan and pour 2 cups water into bottom.  Sprinkle loin liberally with Greek Style sauce.  Mix salt, pepper, oregano and thyme.  Rub well into meat and let stand 20 to 30 minutes.  Place in a 325° oven, bone side up, for 1 hour and 15 minutes.  Turn, add 1 cup of water and roast for 1-1/4 hours more.  Cover roast during last 30 minutes for added tenderness.*

### Method for yams
*Parboil yams, with skins on, in water until slightly firm, approximately 45 minutes.  After removing yams, to this same water add salt, cloves, sugar, orange zest, cinnamon sticks and lemon slice.  Bring water back to a boil, lower to a medium boil for 25 minutes, reducing sauce by half.  Peel yams, cut into 2" squares and place in a roasting pan.  Lay thin slices of butter over yams and pour sugar mixture over.  Sprinkle with vanilla, cinnamon, and nuts.  Bake for 45 minutes at 325° until yams are browned and cooked through.*

# Roasted Pork

# MEATS & POULTRY

## Herb Roasted Chicken with Lemon Garlic Sauce

 *Serves six to eight*

### INGREDIENTS
2 roasting chickens, 3-1/2 lb each
2 tbsp Pappas' extra virgin olive oil
1-1/2 tbsp salt
1 tbsp black pepper
2 heaping tbsp dried Greek oregano
3 cups water
12 to 15 new red potatoes, parboiled
3 oz butter
3 fresh rosemary sprigs

**For lemon garlic sauce**
1 cup fresh lemon juice
1-1/2 cups Pappas' extra virgin olive oil
1/4 to 1/2 cup fresh chopped garlic
1 tsp crushed red pepper
1 medium bunch Italian parsley, stemmed
2 tbsp red wine vinegar
2 tsp salt

*This tangy lemon and garlic sauce, a staple at the Pappas house, is the perfect compliment to roasted chicken or a thick juicy steak. Serve with buttered new potatoes sauteed with fresh rosemary.*

### METHOD
*Rinse chickens thoroughly with cold water. Sprinkle with olive oil and rub with a mixture of oregano, pepper and salt. Pour water into a roasting pan and place chickens in pan, breast side down. Roast in 350° oven for 1 hour and 20 minutes until crispy and brown. When chickens are half cooked, turn and finish with breast side up. Parboil potatoes until just tender and quarter. Saute for about 5 minutes in skillet with melted butter and rosemary sprigs.*

### Method for sauce
*Place all ingredients in blender and process until creamy. For serving, pour small amount over chickens and serve remaining sauce on the side.*

# Herb Roasted Chicken

# MEATS & POULTRY

## Charbroiled Lamb Chops w/ Garlic Mashed Potatoes

 *Serves two*

### INGREDIENTS
8 trimmed french cut rib chops, 1" thick
1/4 cup fresh lemon juice
1/4 cup balsamic vinegar
1/2 cup red wine vinegar
3 cups Pappas' extra virgin olive oil
4 garlic cloves, finely chopped
3 tsp dried Greek oregano
1 tsp salt
1 tsp coarse black pepper

### For garlic mashed potatoes
5 large potatoes
2 cups whole milk
8 oz butter, softened
1 cup yogurt
1/4 cup sour cream
1/2 cup Pappas' extra virgin olive oil
6 large garlic cloves, roasted
3 tsp salt
1 tsp white pepper

*If possible, purchase chops from a young lamb. For an impressive presentation, stand the chops up around creamy garlic mashed potatoes.*

### METHOD
*Lightly salt and pepper the chops. Make a vinaigrette by combining the remaining ingredients in a bowl and whisking until well blended. Place the chops on a charbroiler and baste with vinaigrette while cooking. Brown on both sides until medium rare in center. To serve, baste with vinaigrette and sprinkle with dried Greek oregano and chopped parsley.*

### Method for potatoes
*Boil potatoes, leaving skins on, until tender and remove from pot. Begin mashing potatoes and add butter, salt and pepper. When partially mashed, add milk, yogurt and sour cream. Peel and roast garlic cloves. Place in a blender with olive oil and pulse until smooth. Add to the potatoes and mix until well blended. Season to taste if necessary. Serve while hot. Roasting the garlic cloves before blending mellows the garlic taste.*

# Charbroiled Lamb Chops

# MEATS & POULTRY

## Braised Lamb Shanks
### "Arni Psito"

 Serves two

### INGREDIENTS
4 hind calf lamb shanks, approx. 1 lb each
salt & pepper to coat
dried Greek oregano to coat
1/2 cup Pappas' extra virgin olive oil
2 cups Greek Style sauce to coat (page 48)
2 cups water

### For Spanakorizo
1-1/2 cups uncooked rice
2 lbs fresh spinach
3 cups water
1 cup chopped scallions
1 cup chopped onions
1 tsp dried dill
1/2 tsp fennel seeds
1 tbsp dried mint
1/4 cup Pappas' extra virgin olive oil
1 cup clove honey
1 tsp salt
1/2 tsp pepper
1 stick butter

*Lamb is traditionally the favorite Greek meal. Spanakorizo, spinach flavored rice, is a great modern day accompaniment.*

### METHOD
*Wash lamb shanks thoroughly with cold water. Season lamb well with salt, pepper and oregano. In a roasting pan, over eye burner, sear shanks in hot oil on all sides. Remove roasting pan from burner and sprinkle lamb generously with Greek Style sauce. Add water to bottom of pan. Place pan in 375° oven for 1-1/2 hours, turning occasionally. Remove from oven, add more water if necessary and cover with foil. Continue cooking for about 30 minutes, testing with a fork to ensure doneness.*

### Method for Spanakorizo
*Wash and coarsely chop spinach. Saute scallions and onions in heated butter and oil in a large pot. Add mint, dill, fennel seeds, salt and pepper. Add spinach and rice, mixing well. When spinach is wilted, add water, bring to a light boil, cover and cook 15 to 20 minutes. Remove from heat, fold in honey and keep covered 15 minutes until water is absorbed.*

# Arni Psito

# MEATS & POULTRY

## Chicken Spanaki with Marinara sauce

 *Serves four*

### INGREDIENTS
4 chicken breasts, 8 oz each
1 cup Pappas' extra virgin olive oil
5 pressed garlic cloves
4 cups Spanakopita filling (see page 32)
4 cups rice pilaf (see page 50)
1/2 cup grated Romano cheese

### For Marinara sauce
20 plum tomatoes
1/3 cup Pappas' extra virgin olive oil
1-1/2 cups finely chopped onion
1/4 cup finely chopped garlic
1 tbsp salt
1/2 tsp crushed red pepper
2 cups canned pear tomatoes
1/2 tbsp sugar (if sauce is too tart)
1/4 cup dry red wine
1 cup cold water

*This quickly prepared Marinara sauce should be fresh and never overcooked. Its entire cooking time should not be more than 20 minutes.*

### METHOD
Marinate chicken breasts in mixture of oil and fresh garlic. Grill breasts on char grill until cooked through. Scoop spinach filling onto plate and top with breast. Ladle marinara over chicken and spinach. Serve with rice pilaf and sprinkle plate with cheese.

### Method for Marinara
Seed and coarsely chop the plum tomatoes. In a stock pot, saute onions and garlic in oil until soft. Add plum tomatoes, salt and red pepper. Cook over medium heat 10 minutes until well infused. Reduce heat to low and add sugar, canned tomatoes, and wine. Add water, stir and simmer for additional 5 minutes. Add basil leaves, mix well and remove from heat.

# Chicken Spanaki

## MEATS & POULTRY

## Filet of Tenderloin Milanesa

 *Serves four*

**INGREDIENTS**
4 center cut beef filets, 8 oz each
salt & pepper to taste
2 tbsp chopped fresh garlic
1 cup Pappas' extra virgin olive oil
1-1/2 cups Italian bread crumbs

**For Milanesa sauce**
1 large red bell pepper
1 large yellow bell pepper
1 small green bell pepper
1/2 medium onion
4 oz butter
3/4 tbsp chopped fresh garlic
1/2 cup Chardonnay wine
1/4 cup chicken stock
4 tbsp chopped fresh Italian parsley
1-1/2 cups frozen early peas
3 eggs, hard boiled & coarsely chopped
salt and pepper to taste

*Though certainly not Greek, this delicious Italian recipe is Louie's version of one of Nancy's family favorites.*

**METHOD**
Lightly salt and pepper filets and dip in a mixture of garlic and 1/2 cup olive oil, coating well. Marinate filets for 10 minutes. Remove from marinade and coat well with bread crumbs. In ovenproof skillet, heat the remaining 1/2 cup olive oil until very hot. Slightly flatten filets with your hand and add to skillet. Brown filets about 5 minutes on each side until rare. Drain excess grease, top filets with 1/2 of the Milanesa sauce and place skillet in 375° oven for about 15 minutes, to desired doneness. Plate filets and garnish with balance of Milanesa sauce.

**Method for Milanesa**
Finely chop peppers and onion. Melt butter in a large skillet. Add vegetables, garlic, salt and pepper and cook over medium heat for 5 minutes. Add wine and chicken stock and cook for 3 minutes, until vegetables are crisp tender. Remove from heat, add parsley, peas and chopped eggs. Mix well and set aside.

# Tenderloin Milanesa

# TRADITIONAL GREEK

## Stuffed Grape Leaves
### "Fela or Dolmades"

 *Serves five to six*

This delightful dish is served with Avgolemono, a lemon and egg sauce. Purchase grape leaves packed in brine. After washing leaves, cut the stems to ensure the wraps are tender.

### INGREDIENTS
1-1/2 lb fresh ground beef
3/4 cup uncooked rice
3 ripe tomatoes, finely chopped
1 cup coarsely chopped onions
1 heaping tsp dried mint
1 tsp salt
1/4 tsp white pepper
1/3 cup tomato paste
3/4 cup fresh lemon juice
1/2 cup melted butter
12 cups chicken stock
10 tomato tops
2 lbs pork bones

### METHOD
Place tomatoes, onions, mint, salt and pepper in a bowl. Add beef, rice and tomato paste and mix well. Place a large tablespoon of mix on bottom end of each leaf, roll once, fold in sides and finish roll. In the bottom of a 4 to 6 quart pot, place tomato tops and pork bones and cover with a perforated plate. Place wraps tightly against each other on top. Cover with 4 to 5 flat grape leaves. Mix lemon juice, butter and chicken stock and pour over wraps, covering top layer. Place a heat proof plate on top to prevent unrolling, bring to a boil and reduce to a simmer for 30 minutes until leaves are tender. Remove felas and place on a serving platter, reserving stock for sauce.

### For Avgolemono
1/4 cup chicken bouillon
1 cup cornstarch
3 cups water
3 eggs
juice of 3 large lemons

### Method for Avgolemono
Add bouillon to reserved stock and bring to boil. Remove from heat and slowly add water mixed with cornstarch while stirring. In separate pan beat eggs while slowly adding lemon juice. Slowly combine mixtures while beating.

# Dolmades

# TRADITIONAL GREEK

## Ground Beef w/ Eggplant
### "Mousaka"

 *Serves nine*

### INGREDIENTS
3 medium to large eggplants
3 lbs fresh ground beef
3 tbsp Pappas' extra virgin olive oil
2 cups finely chopped onions
1-1/2 heaping tbsp chopped garlic
1 tbsp salt
1 tbsp white pepper
2 cups water
1 heaping tsp cinnamon
1 cup tomato paste
1/2 cup grated Romano cheese mixed with 1/2 cup grated Kefalotyri cheese
3 cups red vegetable sauce (see page 111)

### For Bechamel topping
6 cups whole milk
1/2 lb butter
3 cups flour
2 eggs
2 cups yogurt      1-1/2 tsp salt
1/2 cup grated Romano cheese mixed with 1/2 cup grated Kefalotyri cheese
1/4 tsp ground nutmeg (optional)

*No Greek cookbook would be complete without Mousaka and this recipe is as traditional as they come.*

### METHOD
*Skin and slice eggplant lengthwise into 1/4" slices. Dip in oil and place on lightly greased sheet pan and bake at 350° for 20 minutes until golden brown. In large pot, saute onions, garlic, salt and pepper in oil until clear. Add beef and water, mixing well and cook over medium heat until beef is almost done. Strain meat to remove excess liquid and return to medium heat. Add cinnamon and tomato paste and cook over low heat until well mixed. In a 9" x 13" pan, layer bottom with eggplant, sprinkle with cheese and top with beef mixture. Repeat, finishing with a layer of eggplant. Top with bechamel and bake at 350° for 40 minutes until golden. Cut into squares, top with grated cheese and red sauce.*

### Method for Bechamel topping
*Bring milk almost to a boil and remove from heat. In separate pan, melt butter and slowly add flour, mixing well, making a heavy roux, then add nutmeg. Remove from heat, add milk, and stir to a thick paste consistency. Fold in eggs, yogurt, salt and cheese mixture. Whisk and mix well.*

# Mousaka

# TRADITIONAL GREEK

## Shish-Ka-Bobs
### "Souvlakia"

 Serves four

### INGREDIENTS
*2 lb pork tenderloin, trimmed*
*3 cups Greek Style sauce (see page 48)*
*2 large red peppers, seeded*
*8 oz fresh mushrooms*
*4 pieces pita bread*
*4 cups rice pilaf (see page 50)*
*1 cup Tzatziki sauce (see page 32)*

*Any visitor to Greece knows the aroma of delicious pork cooked and eaten on skewers along with fresh homemade breads.*

### METHOD
*Cut pork into 1-1/2" squares and place on skewers. Pour 2 cups Greek Style sauce over pork, cover and refrigerate for 1 hour. Cut mushrooms and peppers into bite size pieces, cover with 1 cup Greek Style sauce and refrigerate for 1 hour. Place the pork skewers on char broiler and cook for 20 minutes, rotating occasionally. When half cooked, add peppers and mushrooms to char broiler, turning until brown in color. Butter pita bread and warm both sides on a flat grill. Slice into quarters and line outside of plate. Place a row of rice pilaf down center of plate and lay skewers alongside. Place peppers and mushrooms on the ends. Serve with Tzatziki sauce.*

## Souvlakia

## Baked Macaroni and Meat
## "Pastitso"

 *Serves nine*

### INGREDIENTS
1 lb large penne pasta
3 lbs fresh ground beef
3 tbsp Pappas' extra virgin olive oil
2 cups finely chopped onions
1-1/2 heaping tbsp chopped garlic
1 tbsp salt
1 tbsp white pepper
2 cups water for beef mixture
1 cup tomato paste
1 heaping tsp cinnamon
4 eggs
3/4 cup grated Romano cheese mixed with 3/4 cup grated Kefalotyri cheese
Bechamel topping (see page 82)
red vegetable sauce (see page 111)

*Nancy always says this is a "cheap imitation" of Italian lasagna. Be sure to include the nutmeg in the Bechamel topping for this dish. It compliments the pasta and adds a unique taste.*

### METHOD
*Cook penne until al dente, drain and set aside. In a large pot saute onions, garlic with salt and pepper in oil until clear. Add beef and water, mixing well and cook over medium heat until beef is done. Strain meat to remove excess fat and all liquid and return to medium heat. Add tomato paste and cinnamon and cook over low heat until well mixed. Remove from heat, place in a mixing bowl and let cool a bit. Add unbeaten eggs, pasta and cheese mixture and blend well. Lightly coat a 9" x 13" pan with olive oil, add meat and pasta mixture and pack down until firm. Smooth 1 inch of Bechamel topping over and bake in 350° oven for 40 minutes until golden. Remove from heat, let stand 15 minutes and cut into squares. Sprinkle with grated cheese and serve with red vegetable sauce.*

# Pastitso

# TRADITIONAL GREEK

## Stuffed Vegetables

 *Serves eight*

### INGREDIENTS
1 large zucchini
1 each red, yellow, green bell pepper
3 large tomatoes
1 large eggplant
2 tbsp Pappas' extra virgin olive oil
2 lbs fresh ground beef
1-1/2 cups uncooked rice
1 large tomato, seeded & finely chopped
2 cups finely chopped onion
3 tsp dried mint
2-1/2 tsp salt
1/2 tsp white pepper
1-1/2 cups water
1 tbsp finely chopped fresh garlic
1 heaping tbsp chopped fresh parsley
1 tbsp chicken bouillon
1/2 cup tomato paste
1/4 cup chopped fresh basil
1/2 cup thinly sliced celery
1 cup chicken stock
mix of grated Romano & Kefalotyri cheese
Bechamel sauce (see page 82)
red vegetable sauce (see page 111)

*These vegetables taste as good as they look. You can prepare this recipe using one or all of these vegetables.*

### METHOD
*Cut tops off tomatoes and peppers and remove seeds. Halve zucchini and eggplant. Core each vegetable, taking care not to split the walls. Heat olive oil in a large pot over medium heat and add the ground beef and the next 13 ingredients. You may also chop and add the tops and core of the vegetables. Mix well together and cook uncovered over medium heat approximately 30 to 35 minutes until the rice has soaked up most of the liquid and is soft. Season if necessary, remove from heat and let cool. Generously stuff each of the vegetables up to 1/4" from the top. Pour chicken stock into bottom of a roasting pan. Coat the top of each vegetable with the Bechamel sauce and place in pan. Sprinkle with cheese and paprika. Bake at 350° until tops are golden brown. When skins begin to turn soft, top each with a slice of butter. Serve with red sauce.*

# Stuffed Vegetables

# TRADITIONAL GREEK

## Beef Stew with Onions
### "Stifado"

 *Serves six to eight*

As with many Greek recipes, the flavor of this stew intensifies the longer you cook it. Fresh okra is optional, but we like the color it adds.

### INGREDIENTS
4 lb stew beef, preferably chuck roast
12 large plum tomatoes
3/4 cup Pappas' extra virgin olive oil
10 large garlic cloves, mashed
3 cups cleaned pearl onions
10 oz fresh whole okra, cleaned
1 stick cinnamon, 3" long
2 tbsp salt
1/2 tsp crushed red pepper
4 cups water
1 spring dried Greek oregano, 5" long
2 springs fresh rosemary, 5" long
1 cup red wine vinegar
1 cup tomato paste
1 cup sweet red wine
3 large bay leaves
2 tbsp pickling spice, wrapped in a bag

### METHOD
Cut beef into 2" squares. Cover beef with water in a large stock pot, and boil covered for 5 minutes. Remove from heat, strain and set aside. Cover tomatoes with water and boil until skins begin to split, about 3 to 5 minutes. Remove from heat, peel and seed. Mash tomatoes with a whisk. In a large stew pot, brown garlic in oil over medium heat. Add salt, cinnamon and red pepper and saute for 15 seconds. Add tomatoes, onions and okra and stew for 5 minutes. Add water, rosemary, oregano and vinegar, mixing well. Add beef and bring to a boil then reduce to a simmer. Add tomato paste, wine, bay leaves and pickling spice. Cover and continue to simmer until meat is tender, approximately 1 hour. For a sweeter stew, you may add a little sugar. Serve while hot.

# Stifado

# TRADITIONAL GREEK

## Lamb Stew
### "Arni Fasolakia"

 Serves four to six

*A winter favorite, lamb stew's popularity has withstood the seasons of time and the ever changing tastes of the American palate.*

### INGREDIENTS
5 hind lamb shanks, approx. 1 lb each
salt and pepper
1 cup Pappas' extra virgin olive oil
1/2 cup flour
3 heaping tbsp chopped garlic
2 cups finely chopped onions
1 cup chopped celery
1 cup chopped carrots
3/4 cup chopped Italian parsley
4 large bay leaves
1/2 yellow bell pepper, chopped
1/2 red bell pepper, chopped
1 tbsp coarse black pepper
1 tbsp salt
1/2 cup crushed fresh tomatoes with skins
1-1/2 cups tomato paste
8 cups water
1 lb fresh string beans

### METHOD
Have butcher cut shanks in half crosswise. Salt and pepper shanks and cook in 1/2 cup hot oil in a three gallon stew pot for 3 minutes on each side. Remove from heat and discard fat and oil. Place pot back on high heat with shanks and add 1/2 cup oil, flour, 1 cup water, garlic and onions. Mix well and cook for an additional 5 minutes, stirring occasionally. Add the celery, carrots, parsley, bay leaves, peppers, salt and black pepper. Add crushed tomatoes, tomato paste and 8 cups water, mixing well. Cover and cook over low to medium heat 1 hour and 20 minutes. Clean and remove tips from string beans and add during the last 30 minutes of cooking. Check shanks with a fork for tenderness. Remove from heat and serve.

# Arni Fasolakia

# BREADS & DESSERTS

## Louis Pappas' Greek Bread & Dipping Oil

 *Makes three loaves*

### INGREDIENTS
3 lbs bread baking flour
3 tsp salt
3 tsp sugar
4 tsp shortening
3-1/2 cups water
5 tsp yeast
pinch of baking powder

### For dipping oil
2 cups chopped Italian parsley
1 cup chopped curly parsley
1/4 cup finely chopped garlic
1/4 cup red wine vinegar
1/4 cup balsamic vinegar
3/4 cup fresh sweet basil
1 tsp crushed red pepper
2 tbsp dried Greek oregano
1 tsp fresh thyme
1 tbsp salt
2/3 cup finely grated Romano cheese
2/3 cup Pappas' extra virgin olive oil

*This bread recipe was created by Louis Pappas in 1925. The dipping oil was inspired by grandson Louis Pappas to satisfy changing tastes.*

### METHOD
*Blend all bread ingredients in a large mixer. Form into three long loaves. Cover with a cloth and let proof for 45 minutes. They should double in size. Bake in 325° oven for 40 minutes until they reach a golden brown crust. Wipe tops of loaves with clean damp cloth for a nice glow.*

### Method for dipping oil
*Combine all ingredients in a food processor to chop and blend. Sauce will last several weeks in refrigerator. To serve, place small amount of sauce on plate and add Pappas' extra virgin olive oil for dipping. Makes 4 cups.*

# Greek Bread & Dipping Oil

# BREADS & DESSERTS

## Kalamata Olive Raisin Bread

 *Makes three loaves*

### INGREDIENTS
3 lbs bread baking flour
3 tsp salt
3 tsp sugar
1-1/2 cups seeded and chopped
    Kalamata olives
3/4 cup raisins
1/2 cup Pappas' extra virgin olive oil
4 tsp shortening
3-1/2 cups water
5 tsp yeast
pinch of baking powder

*This is one of Louie's many new creations. The saltiness of the olives combined with the sweetness of the raisins gives this bread a uniquely interesting taste.*

### METHOD
Blend all bread ingredients in a large mixer. Form into three long loaves. Cover with a cloth and let proof for 45 minutes. They should double in size. Bake in 325° oven for 40 minutes until they reach a golden brown crust. Wipe tops of loaves with clean damp cloth for a nice glow.

# Kalamata Olive Bread

## Mama Pappas' Rice Pudding

### "Rizogalo"

 *Makes twelve servings*

This is the original recipe created by Mama Pappas when the Riverside Cafe was first opened in 1925.

### INGREDIENTS
4 cups washed rice
3 quarts milk
3 cups sugar
2 cinnamon sticks
1/4 cup vanilla extract
3 oz butter
5 eggs
cinnamon

### METHOD
Cook washed rice, keeping covered with water, at a hard boil for 10 to 15 minutes. Drain and set aside. In a large pot, heat milk. Add the rice, sugar, cinnamon sticks, vanilla extract and butter. Bring to a boil then reduce to a light boil. Stir frequently with a wooden spoon, making sure rice does not stick to bottom of pan. Cook until rice is completely done, approximately 40 minutes. Once rice is cooked, remove from heat. Crack the eggs in a separate pot and beat well. Slowly add 5 ladles of rice mixture, stirring continuously. Slowly pour back into main rice mixture. Serve hot or cold. Sprinkle with cinnamon and garnish with a cinnamon stick or a vanilla wafer.

# Mama's Rice Pudding

# BREADS & DESSERTS

## Galaktoboureko

 Serves nine

### INGREDIENTS
2 qts milk
4 tbsp butter
1-1/4 cups sugar
2 small egg yolks
1-1/2 cups cream of wheat
1 lb phyllo sheets
ground cinnamon

### For simple syrup
1 cup sugar
1-1/2 cups water
juice of 1 lemon
2 cinnamon sticks
1 tbsp vanilla extract

*"Gala", which means milk in Greek, contributes to the thick creamy texture of this enticing dessert.*

### METHOD
*Butter 9" x 13" baking pan and line with 6 to 8 phyllo sheets, buttering each sheet until you have a 6 inch overlap outside of pan. Bring milk, butter and sugar to a simmer while stirring. Beat egg yolks and blend into mixture. In a steady stream, slowly add cream of wheat to hot milk. Stir and cook slowly over medium heat for 6 to 8 minutes until slightly thickened. Pour mixture into lined pan and fold all overlapping phyllo inward. Butter each remaining phyllo sheet well and cover top of pan, tucking in edges. With a sharp knife, cut into thirds lengthwise, cutting through to the bottom. Bake in 325° oven for 30 to 45 minutes until cooked through and phyllo is browned. Pour syrup liberally over scores and sides, soaking thoroughly. Let stand for 2 hours. Cut into squares and sprinkle with cinnamon.*

### Method for syrup
*Combine water, sugar, cinnamon sticks and lemon juice, bring to a boil and cook for 10 minutes. Remove from heat, add vanilla and blend well.*

# Galaktoboureko

# BREADS & DESSERTS

## Baklava

 Serves fifteen to eighteen

Baklava is a rich and delicate Greek pastry, considered an outstanding special occasion dessert. Making the phyllo dough takes hours, therefore purchasing it is entirely acceptable.

### INGREDIENTS
1 lb phyllo dough (about 14 sheets)
1 cup finely ground pecans
1 cup coarsely chopped walnuts
    or pecans
1/2 cup sugar
1 lb butter, melted
1 cup blanched almonds, chopped
1/2 cup crushed Zwieback
1 tsp cinnamon

### For syrup
4 cups granulated sugar
1 tbsp lemon juice
2 cups water

Bring the water and sugar to a boil, stirring until all sugar is dissolved. Allow to boil for about 5 minutes more. Remove from heat and add the lemon juice.

### METHOD
Brush a 9" x 13" baking dish with melted butter and place a sheet of the phyllo in the bottom allowing the dough to overlap on all sides. Brush dough with butter. Place five more sheets of phyllo on top of this layer, brushing each with butter, leaving excess phyllo over sides of pan. Mix almonds, pecans and walnuts and add the Zwieback, sugar and cinnamon. Sprinkle the phyllo with a layer of this mixture, place two more sheets of phyllo on top of this, brushing the phyllo generously with butter. Repeat this process until the nut mixture is used up. Fold in excess from sides and place two or three layers of phyllo on top, brushing with butter. Cut the cake into serving pieces to ensure baking of all ingredients. Bake at 375° for 1 hour, checking for browning. Remove from oven, let cool and pour warm syrup over.

# Baklava

# BREADS & DESSERTS

## Greek Doughnuts
### "Loukoumades"

 *Makes three dozen*

*You can always find Loukoumades at a Greek Festival or Church Bazaar. Prepare them at home for a delicious family treat.*

### INGREDIENTS
*2 cups bread flour*
*1 tbsp yeast*
*1 tsp salt*
*1 tsp sugar*
*1-3/4 cups water*
*juice of 1 orange*
*blended oil for frying*
*clove honey*
*ground cinnamon*

### METHOD
*Blend flour, yeast, salt and sugar together. While stirring constantly, slowly add the water, making a thick consistency. Cover with a towel and place in a warm place for 30 minutes. After mixture has risen, add the juice of the orange and whisk well. Heat about 4 inches of oil in a pot until very hot. Take a large spoonful of mixture and carefully drop into hot oil. Continue dropping spoonfuls of the mixture, taking care not to overcrowd the pot. When doughnuts are brown on one side, turn and brown the other side. Drain on paper towels to remove excess oil. Drizzle doughnuts with honey and sprinkle with cinnamon.*

# Loukoumades

## BREADS & DESSERTS

# Fig & Guava Phyllo Pastry

 *Makes eight servings*

*This tropical Greek hybrid can be folded traditionally into triangles or free form for a much prettier presentation.*

### INGREDIENTS
*8 oz dried figs*
*1/2 cup water*
*3 oz butter*
*1 tsp ground cinnamon*
*1/4 cup sugar*
*1/3 cup guava paste*
*1/8 cup finely chopped walnuts*
*1/8 cup Creme de Casis*
*2 tbsp brandy*
*8 oz cream cheese*
*phyllo dough*
*1 cup melted butter*

### For fig topping
*Combine 1 cup of fig mixture with 3/4 cup heavy cream. Mix well over medium heat stirring constantly, until you have a smooth, pourable consistency.*

### METHOD
*Finely chop figs in a blender and add to a large skillet with the water. Cook over medium heat until most water is gone to soften figs. Add butter, sugar, cinnamon, guava paste and nuts. Mix well and cook for 5 minutes. Increase heat, add Creme de Casis and brandy and flame. Cook, stirring constantly, for 5 minutes while alcohol burns off. Remove from heat, add cream cheese and blend until well mixed. Reserve 1 cup of mixture to make topping.*

*For free form: Lightly butter one sheet of phyllo and scrunch it up to form a flower shape with a pocket in the middle. Place 1 large tablespoon of fig filling in pocket and top with one sheet of lightly buttered phyllo in the same shape.*
*For traditional form: Lightly butter phyllo sheets and fold the same way as Spanakopita. (see page 32)*

*Bake at 350° until all layers are golden. To serve, pour fig topping over and sprinkle with cinnamon. Add vanilla ice cream if desired.*

# Fig & Guava Phyllo

## Aunt Pauline's Greek Wedding Cookies
### "Karithota"

 *Makes fifty cookies*

Although Kourambiethes are more commonly prepared for weddings, we prefer this version which is much more buttery and contains more nuts.

**INGREDIENTS**
1 lb butter
8 tbsp powdered sugar
3-1/2 cups chopped pecans
4 cups flour
2 tbsp vanilla extract
2 tbsp ice water
1 lb powdered sugar

**METHOD**
Cream the butter thoroughly and add the 8 tbsp of powdered sugar. Continue creaming until well blended. Mix the pecans with the flour and gradually add to the butter and sugar mixture. Add the vanilla and ice water and mix well. Roll dough with palm of hand into half moon designs or 1 inch rolls. Place on cookie sheets and bake in 350° oven until golden brown. Sift powdered sugar generously over cookies.

# Karithota

# SAUCES

## Brown Lamb Sauce or Brown Beef Sauce

 *Makes two to three quarts*

*This sauce, made with lamb, can also be made for beef by replacing the lamb tips and bouillon with beef bones and beef bouillon. Lamb bouillon can be found at gourmet shops. The longer you cook it, the heartier the flavor.*

### INGREDIENTS
*5 lbs lamb shank tips, bone in
(or 5 lbs beef bones in 2" cuts)
1/3 cup Pappas' extra virgin olive oil
1 gallon water
1 large onion
2 large carrots
1 large green bell pepper
4 celery stems with leaves
1 small bunch Italian parsley
1 tbsp chopped garlic
8 heaping tbsp lamb bouillon
(or 8 heaping tbsp beef bouillon)
3 tbsp Kitchen Bouquet*

### METHOD
*In a large stock pot, brown shank tips (or beef bones) in oil. Cut vegetables into chunks and add them to pot with parsley and garlic. Mix well and cook approximately 10 minutes until vegetables soften. Add water and bring to a hard boil. Reduce to a light boil, cover and simmer for 1 hour. Uncover, add bouillon and Kitchen Bouquet and cook for an additional hour, reducing sauce by 1/3. Mash vegetables while straining sauce through a fine mesh strainer. Thicken with cornstarch if necessary.
Note: If cooking lamb, reserve all drippings for use instead of bouillon.*

# SAUCES

## Red Vegetable Sauce

 *Makes two to three quarts*

This sauce is delicious served over Mousaka, Pastitso and other casseroles or quite simply over rice or pasta.

### INGREDIENTS
4 firm tomatoes
3 celery stems
1 medium carrot
1 medium white onion
1 large green bell pepper
10 large garlic cloves, halved
1/8 cup pickling spice
1/4 cup salt
1 gallon water
1/4 cup chicken bouillon
1 cup tomato paste
1 cup chili sauce
1 cup ketchup
1 cup cornstarch
3 cups water

### METHOD
Cut vegetables into chunks and place in a two gallon stock pot with garlic, pickling spice, chicken bouillon and salt. Add 1 gallon of water and bring to a hard boil. Reduce to a medium boil and add tomato paste, chili sauce and ketchup, stirring until tomato paste is dissolved. Cook an additional 25 minutes then remove from heat. Mash vegetables while straining sauce through a fine mesh strainer. Thoroughly mix cornstarch with 3 cups water and slowly add to the sauce while stirring to thicken sauce if necessary.

# INDEX

**APPETIZERS**
Bruschetta with feta cheese, 20
Eggplant, fried, 30
Eggplant, roasted spread
  (melitzanosalata), 26
Grouper, Caribbean wraps, 28
Hummus, 26
Kalamata olive spread, 26
Octopus, marinated, 22
Saganaki, flaming, 24
Spanakopita, 32
Tridopita, 32
Zucchini, fried, 30

**BREAD**
Greek, 94
Kalamata olive raisin, 96

**CHEESE**
Kaseri, 36
Kefalotyri, 24, 82, 86, 88
Mizithra, 36, 38
Saganaki, flaming, 24

**DESSERTS**
Baklava, 102
Cookies, Greek wedding
  (karithota), 108
Doughnuts (loukoumades), 104
Fig & guava phyllo pastry, 106
Galaktoboureko, 100
Rice pudding (rizogalo), 98

**MEATS & POULTRY**
Beef
  filet of tenderloin Milanesa, 78
  ground, with eggplant
    (mousaka), 82
  ground, with macaroni
    (pastitso), 86
  prime rib, 66
  stew, with onions (stifado), 90
Chicken
  egg lemon soup
    (avgolemono soupa), 8
  herb roasted w/ lemon garlic, 70
  spanaki with marinara, 76

**MEATS & POULTRY (cont'd)**
Lamb
  chops, charbroiled, 72
  roast leg of (arni sto fourno), 64
  shanks, braised (arni psito), 74
  stew (arni fasolakia), 92
Pork
  roasted with yams, 68
  shish-ka-bobs (souvlakia), 84

**PASTAS**
Clams Chardonnay w/ sundried
  tomato cream sauce, 40
Greek pasta salad, 18
Halkitika macaronia, 36
Seafood, 34
Shrimp & feta cheese, 38

**RICE**
Pilaf, 50
Pudding, 98
Spanakorizo, 74

**SALADS**
Bahamian conch, 16
Greek, famous, 12
Greek pasta, 18
Potato, 12
Village (horiatiki), 14

**SAUCES**
Avgolemono, 80
Bechamel, 82
Bread, dipping, 94
Brown, beef or lamb, 110
Greek style, 48
Greek yogurt, 52
Lemon garlic, 70
Marinara, 76
Milanesa, 78
Red vegetable, 111
Tzatziki, 32

**SEAFOOD**
Clams, Chardonnay w/ sundried
  tomato cream sauce, 40
Clams, seafood pasta, 34

**SEAFOOD (cont'd)**
Conch
  Bahamian salad, 16
  pan fried Bahamian cracked, 46
Grouper
  3rd generation, 56
  Aegean, 50
  Caribbean wraps, 28
  grilled w/ Greek style sauce, 48
Mussels, seafood pasta, 34
Octopus
  charbroiled, 54
  marinated, 22
Salmon spanaki, 58
Scallops
  pan seared w/ yogurt sauce, 52
  seafood pasta, 34
Seafood pasta, 34
Shrimp
  butter pan fried, 42
  feta pasta, with, 38
  peppered, 60
  seafood pasta, 34
  u-peel 'em, 42
Snapper, red, fire grilled, 44
Squid, baby, butter pan fried, 62

**SOUPS & STEWS**
Beef with onions (stifado), 90
Chicken, egg & lemon
  (avgolemono soupa) 8
Lamb (arni fasolakia), 92
Tomato orzo, 10

**SPREADS**
Eggplant, roasted
  (melitzanosalata), 26
Hummus, 26
Kalamata olive, 26

**TRADITIONAL GREEK**
Arni fasolakia (lamb stew), 92
Arni psito (lamb shanks), 74
Arni sto fourno (leg of lamb), 64
Avgolemono soupa (chicken,
  egg & lemon soup), 8

**TRADITIONAL GREEK (cont'd)**
Dolmades or fela (stuffed
  grape leaves), 80
Galaktoboureko, 100
Halkitika macaronia, 36
Horiatiki (village) salata, 14
Kalamarakia (baby squid), 62
Karithota (wedding cookies), 108
Loukoumades (doughnuts), 104
Mousaka (ground beef with
  eggplant), 82
Rizogalo (rice pudding), 98
Pastito (ground beef with
  macaroni), 86
Stifado (beef stew), 90
Souvlakia (shish-ka-bobs), 84
Spanakopita & Tiropita, 32

**VEGETABLES**
Eggplant
  fried, 30
  ground beef, with, 82
  roasted spread
    (melitzanosalata), 26
  stuffed, 88
Onion rings, shoe string, 66
Peppers, stuffed, 88
Potatoes
  garlic mashed, 72
  Greek style oven brown, 64
  salad, 12
  skordalia, 30
Spinach
  chicken spanaki, 76
  salmon spanaki, 58
  spanakopita, 32
  spanakorizo, 74
Tomatoes
  orzo soup, and, 10
  stuffed, 88
Yams, 68
Zucchini
  fried, 30
  stuffed, 88

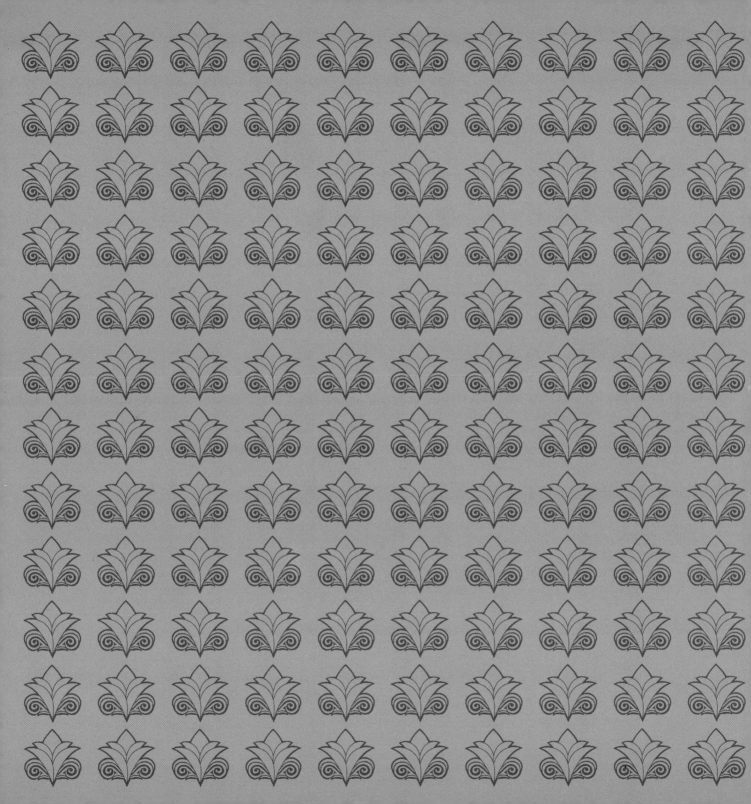